YOUR KNOWLEDGE HAS VALUE

Culture in disguise. Congo's impact on New Orleans voodoo

Lisa Turan

Bibliographic information published by the German National Library:

The German National Library lists this publication in the National Bibliography; detailed bibliographic data are available on the Internet at http://dnb.dnb.de.

ISBN: 9783346919298
This book is also available as an ebook.

© GRIN Publishing GmbH
Trappentreustraße 1
80339 München

Print and binding: Books on Demand GmbH, Norderstedt, Germany
Printed on acid-free paper from responsible sources.

The present work has been carefully prepared. Nevertheless, authors and publishers do not incur liability for the correctness of information, notes, links and advice as well as any printing errors.

GRIN web shop: https://www.grin.com/document/1379696

University of H.

Faculty of History

Introduction to African History (seminar)

"A culture in disguise –Kongo's impact on New Orleans's voodoo"

18th August 2022

Lisa Turan

Main subject: Education (Sek. I/II)

1. Minor: English

2. Minor: History

Contents:

Introduction   1

1. Conceptualization of "New Orleans Voodoo"   2

2. Kongo's religious movements from the 13th to 17th century   3

3. Transatlantic slave trade between Central Africa and North America   4

4. Kongolese slaves and the development of voodoo in New Orleans   6

5. Elements of Kongo religiosity in New Orleans Voodoo   8

Conclusion   12

Works Cited   13

A culture in disguise –Kongo's impact on New Orleans's voodoo

Since the first enslaved Africans had reached the coast of Virginia in 1619, European, American, and African slave traders captured about one-quarter of all African slaves in Central Africa to ship them to the Americas via the Congo River or other ports along the Congolese Loango due to the transatlantic slave trade (Voss 40). Significantly, these enslaved people, mostly from the Kongo regions, did not solely bring a free workforce, but also a huge cultural heritage that shaped the American culture (Cooksey et al. 4). Likewise, these slaves practiced African religiosity despite the established Catholicism by Europeans in the Americas (Cooksey et al. 9). Out of this blending of African religiosity with Christianity developed the Afro American syncretism today known as "voodoo". Widely unknown is the immense influence of Kongo religiosity on voodoo due to slave imports from Kongo to New Orleans. Accordingly, this leads to the question, which elements of Kongolese religiosity originate within New Orleans Voodoo due to the transatlantic slave trade?

In this regard, I begin with the conceptualization of New Orleans Voodoo as a distinct branch of Haitian Vodou, followed by an overview of religious movements from the pre-and early colonial period of Kongo to understand the religious fundaments of this paper. To comprehend the connections between the transatlantic slave trade and the emergence of Kongolese religiosity despite slavery in New Orleans, I will firstly provide data on slave imports from Central Africa to North America. Secondly, I analyze the increase of the Kongolese slave population and the uncommon slavery conditions in Louisiana that contributed to the development of New Orleans Voodoo. Finally, I detect the resulting parallels of Kongolese religiosity that can be found in the voodoo of New Orleans. To cover the broad spectrum of the research field, I will evaluate the secondary literature of various scholars, among others Wyatt MacGaffey, Jelmer Voss, Daniel da Silva, Jerah Johnson, Astrid Reuter, Blake Touchstone, and Ina Fandrich, to discuss their theories and concepts.

1. CONCEPTUALIZATION OF "NEW ORLEANS VOODOO"

To discover Kongolese roots in New Orleans Voodoo, it is primarily important to understand the religion's key elements. Despite the close relationship between Haitian Vodou and New Orleans Voodoo, this section focuses on the conceptualization of New Orleans Voodoo to create a common framework for the following research paper.

Voodoo is often used for a broad variety of concepts and is difficult to define. Comprehensively, the term "voodoo" refers to an African American syncretism originating in religious beliefs from West Central Africa that were orally conveyed to North America due to the transatlantic slave trade (Mattes 580). The religion has no holy scripture and is closely linked to other Latin American syncretism, such as the Haitian Vodou (Fandrich 786), Afro Brazilian Candomblé, or the Cuban Santeria (Mattes 580). Linguistically, "voodoo" derives from the Fon word "vodou" and means "spirit" or "deity" (Britannica Marie Laveau).

In general, New Orleans Voodoo practitioners believe in a spiritual hierarchy with the highest god "Li Grand Zombi" and a pantheon of "loa" spirits, spirits of the dead, and saints (Fandrich 786). The word "loa" originates in the Fon word "lwa" and means "god" or "secret" (Mattes 582). Loas intend to keep the balance between gods, humans, and ancestors (Lademann-Priemer 426). Furthermore, loas either belong to the "Rada" or the "Pedro" cult of voodoo (De Heusch 290).

Moreover, voodoo is a possession cult in which priests or priestesses initiate rituals, including sacrifices and trances, to connect practitioners with the gods and relieve them from problems or demonic illnesses (Mattes 583). One significant voodoo priestess of New Orleans was Marie Laveau who lived during the 19th century and is believed to have had healing powers (Britannica Marie

Laveau). Aside from rituals, she used "gris-gris" (charms) to achieve fortune for her clients or misfortune for their enemies (Touchstone 373). The black and white community consulted her likewise (Britannica Marie Laveau).

The conceptualization of New Orleans Voodoo portrays the religion's main aspects. To recognize Kongolese influences within its practices, I will now draw the line from voodoo religiosity to religious movements of the Kongo kingdom.

2. KONGO'S RELIGIOUS MOVEMENTS FROM 13TH to 17TH CENTURY

The Kongo kingdom experienced various religious movements over the centuries. For brevity, I will mainly focus on the religiosity of "The old kingdom" (13th to 17th century) in this chapter.

The term "Kongo" refers to the western Congo Republic, Cabinda in Angola, and the lower part of the Zaire Republic (MacGaffey ix). The population called "BaKongo" lived in small communities (195). They believed in cosmology, which means that the world and the universe are holistic, and structured in space and time, with hierarchies between gods and humans, and the living and dead (3). The systems further served as a social, political, and economic basis (4). Within these communities, kings and priests were the most influential persons (197). Many aspects of Kongo religiosity such as the assemblage of chief and priests in official functions or the worship of rocks and waters remained stable until the 20th century (197).

The Portuguese encountered the Kongo kingdom in 1485. According to their world view, the BaKongo people interpreted them as visitors to the land of the dead and were extraordinarily excited to welcome their religiosity (199). When King Nzinga Nkuwu was baptized in 1491, he restricted the new cult to a small number of chiefs within his community, but the demand increased when Christianity became a new approach for the Kongo society to achieve higher powers (200) The king quit Christianity two years later, but his eldest son Afonso I, a baptized Christian, became his successor and established Christianity in Kongo and integrated Christian rites into Kongolese religious practices (200).

So far, the above shows the religious change from Kongolese religiosity during the pre-and colonial era until the emergence of Christianity by the arrival of the Portuguese peoples in Kongo. In this regard, it is worth emphasizing the familiarity of the Christian faith among the BaKongo people before the transatlantic slave trade. It is hard to avoid the conclusion that Christianity already blended in with Kongolese rituals and practices before the enslavement and arrival of Kongolese slaves in Catholic Louisiana. However, questions about the role of Christianity cannot be taken into consideration within this research.

3. TRANSATLANTIC SLAVE TRADE BETWEEN CENTRAL AFRICA AND NORTH AMERICA

The transatlantic slave trade had very profound effects on the development of American religiosity. The third chapter illustrates economic explanations, figures of African captives, and significant embarkment locations of West and Central Africa to discover the reasons for the vast number of slaves from the Kongo kingdom in New Orleans.

The transatlantic slave trade between Europe, Africa, and the Americas began when the first twenty enslaved Africans, in all likelihood captives from Kongo, reached the coast of Virginia in 1619 (Voss 40). Europeans bought most of their slaves solely from West Africa during the second half of the 17th century (Domingues Da Silva 22). However, when the tobacco, rice, and indigo economy accelerated significantly in 1676 and the workforce in the Americas became more and more obligatory for African slaves (Voss 41), they started to purchase slaves additionally from independent Central African slave traders near the Congo River (22). The main Western Central African slave trading port on the African coast was Luanda in Portuguese Angola, but most of the sold slaves of Luanda came from the African backlands and the Kongo kingdom (40), which was a flourishing area for captives because conflicts between the local Kongo monarchies and European military (Cooksey et al. 9).

The number of Kongo slaves further increased when Kongo enacted the peace agreement in 1709 to end their civil war, which resulted in political unrest and tremendous growth of enslavement of political opponents, their followers, other criminals as well as children (Voss 45). During the 1730s, Central African captives were mainly shipped to Charleston, the new anchor point for the slave trade (33). During that time, 90,000 out of 106,000 slaves survived the Middle Passage voyage to North America, and one-third of those slaves left Africa by one of the main harbors along the Congo River or Loango Coast, such as Cabinda or Malembo (43). Subsequently, they were moved to the Southern regions of North America as the new hotspot areas for cotton plantation labor (44). According to the "Voyages Database", about 2.8 million West Central African slaves came to North America from 1781 to 1867 (Domingues Da Silva 19). The rising import of African slaves from various areas had more and more influence on the religious developments of American society (Voss 43).

By the end of the 17th century, industrialization in Europe fueled the enor-mous demand for tobacco, rice, cotton, and sugar (Domingues Da Silva 16). By that time, the Congo River became by far the most significant market for Britain and American slave traders, with captives from Gabon, Malebo Pool, the Kongo kingdom, and the Angolan hinterland (Voss 45). Luanda remained another major trading area with ports such as Ambriz and Loango, among others (Domingues Da Silva 32). Additionally, warlords from Luanda and Luba sold high amounts of Western Central Africans (18).

Nevertheless, the moral perception of slavery among Europeans and Americans began to change with the Haitian Revolution in 1791 (37). The suc-cessful abolition of slavery and the independence of Haiti from France in 1804 (Reuter 30) were conducted by European and American abolitionist movements (Domingues Da Silva 16). Even though Florida and New Orleans continued to smuggle more than 5,000 slaves from the Congo River illegally into the US (Voss 43), slaving activities in western Central Africa decreased, especially after the slave trade abolition by Britain in 1807 and the abolition of slavery by the US in 1808 (24).

The above figures validate that West and Central Africa were fruitful areas for slave traders to capture humans predominantly from the Kongo regions due to the growing demand for the slave labor force. During the 17th and 18th centuries, the growing number of African slaves contributed to the Africanization of Southern North America and implied religiosity that eventually blended in with European values. The next section focuses on the influences of slaves from Kongo on New Orleans to understand the development of New Orleans Voodoo.

4. KONGOLESE SLAVES AND THE DEVELOPMENT OF VOODOO IN NEW ORLEANS

Thinking of slavery in the Americas generally leads to the presumption of strict suppression and exploitation of African Americans. The question at this point is how Kongo religiosity could become the fundament of New Orleans Voodoo despite strict slave conditions. Within the following section, I will find answers to the question by examining the circumstances of slavery in Louisiana and the effects of Kongolese migrants on New Orleans's Voodoo.

When France colonized Louisiana in 1699, the population of the new territory suffered from starvation (Johnson 121). In 1719, when the first African slaves reached Louisiana (Long 87), plantation owners were barely capable to feed themselves and even less their slaves (Johnson 121). Hence, plantation owners handed over pieces of their land to slaves and allowed them free weekends to culture their crops and feed themselves (122) unsupervised (124). Unlike any other Southern region, French Louisiana achieved a milestone for Afro-American slaves that provided space for the development of African religiosity in North America despite slavery.

Shortly after the establishment of free days for slaves, they began to trade agricultural surplus and other necessities on square markets in New Orleans (122). One of the city's most famous square markets became later known as "Congo Square". Back then, this place was a popular meeting spot for the Afro-American community (131). Notably, the name of the market implies a huge amount of Kongolese slaves in New Orleans. Afro-Americans gathered there for religious practicing including singing, dancing, and playing drums, which the French government permitted during that time (Long 89). Catholicism and other religious mixtures merged into the earliest form of New Orleans Voodoo (87). When Louisiana became Spanish in 1762, the importation of slaves from Kongo accelerated significantly (Dewulf 26). Under Spanish rule, 20 percent of African captives came from Kongo and supported the adoption of Kongolese culture and religiosity within American society (Fandrich 786).

When rebellious African slaves fought for the abolition of slavery during the Haitian Revolution (1791 to 1804), many black inhabitants fled the isle due to economic instability and political unrest (Britannica Haitian Revolution). As a result, 10,000 Haitian refugees moved to New Orleans which affected the city's religious practices (Fandrich 786). Many refugees followed Haitian Vodou, which was said to be the religion that empowered the Haitian rebellions to kill their masters during their fight for freedom (Mattes 582). However, the New Orleans community already developed its religious practices (Fandrich 785). Eventually, a mixture of Haitian Vodou and New Orleans religiosity merged into the New Orleans Voodoo (786) that had been manifested by free and enslaved Afro Americans (Britannica Haitian Revolution). When Louisiana was sold to North America in 1803 (Fandrich 780), New Orleans's mixture of languages and religions, and the loose slave conditions were unbearable for the new government (Long 97) and resulted in the suppression of Afro Americans and the condemnation of voodoo (87). Finally, voodoo-practicing decreased and could only be held secretly (Touchstone 377).

This historical approach to reconstructing slave conditions in French and Spanish Louisiana allows potential insights into matters that are in fact both, interesting and important. Because the European governments of Louisiana had allowed easier slave conditions, there was certainly space for religious progression from the African diaspora. Accordingly, slaves from Kongo were able to practice their traditions and rituals freely, at least to some extent, which effectively shaped the religious fundament for New Orleans Voodoo. Doubtlessly, an entirely different conception grew up under the North American government and their stricter slavery measures, nevertheless, the religious basis of New Orleans Voodoo had

been established. Consequently, I will detect similarities between Kongolese religiosity and New Orleans Voodoo in the next chapter.

5. ELEMENTS OF KONGO RELIGIOSITY IN NEW ORLEANS VOODOO

Integrally combined with the above, I proved that the transatlantic slave trade was
the main indicator for the increase in Kongolese people in New Orleans that, in
addition to less strict slave conditions than elsewhere in the South, forwarded
New Orleans Voodoo. Eventually, I will return to the key question of this paper
and find actual evidence for components of Kongolese religiosity that are rooted
within New Orleans Voodoo.

As shortly introduced in chapter 2, the pre-colonial BaKongo people believed in cosmology. They interpreted the world as one holistic entity, within
which humans were one of many components structured in a system of time and
space (MacGaffey 5). They believed in "reciprocating" and "spiritual" universes,
of which the second will be closely examined in this paper (6).

Within the spiritual universe, gods, spirits, humans, and the dead exist in
hierarchically divided spheres (46). On top of the sky lives "Nzambi", the highest
god and creator of the universe who hardly intervenes in human actions (78).
Nzambi is represented by subordinated natural spirits (80). The next in line are local spirits, who live in spheres such as the land, waters (75), forests, crossings, or
cemeteries (6) and live side by side with ancestors, ghosts, and charms on the
same level (75). They are followed by priests, chiefs, magicians, witches, and el-
ders, and ranked together with children, grandchildren, and other "nzambis (humans) of the world of the living on the lowest rank (75). The dead belong to the
underground world (46).

New Orleans Voodoo practitioners adopted a very similar spiritual system
into their practices. According to their belief, "Li Grand Zombi" is the highest god
who lives separately from the pantheon of subordinated "loa" spirits, saints, and
the spirits of the dead (Fandrich 786). The word "zombie" derives from "nzambi"
in the Kikongo language (786). Like in Kongo cosmology, firstly, the highest

voodoo god does not intervene in human activities (Reuter 36), and secondly, Li Grand Zombi's inferior loas rest in waters, forests, street crossings, or other spheres (Mattes 582) similarly to the local spirits of the Kongo cosmos. One important deity is "Papa Elegba", the mediating loa between gods and humans, who watches the entrance of temples and keeps dark magic away (Reuter 35). Likewise, his character relates to a Kongolese Christian Saint named "Anthony of Padua" (Fandrich 787), which proves, despite not from a cosmological perspective, the Kongolese origins.

Another resemblance can be seen between Kongo's concept of the world of the dead and New Orleans's death cult. Regarding Kongo cosmology, the spiritual universe has two co-existing worlds for the living and the dead (MacGaffey 6). The BaKongo believed that humans transcend the state of life and death in one endless circle (44). After death, humans become a ghost of the land of the dead (45). However, healers can bring them back from the world of the dead. This passing is called "lufwa" (53). Other members of the world of the dead are ancestors, and local and natural spirits (8). They are separated from the living by waters (43) and might reside in forests or cemeteries (55). Sunset symbolizes death, but sunrise symbolizes rebirth (43). Both worlds flip with each other during nighttime and the dead walk around in their human appearance (48).

New Orleans Voodoo exerts a strong death cult (Fandrich 786). Aside from burying deaths in rituals, they believe in "zombies" who represent dead souls in the sphere of the living (Mattes 582). As already discussed, the term "zombie" derives from the Kikongo word "nzambi" (Fandrich 786). The BaKongo presumption of deaths who return and move in human appearance to the world of the living reminds us of modern New Orleans zombies. Although voodoo believers honor dead souls, they fear becoming zombies by themselves and in connection to that, being submissive to a master, which reveals anxieties of previous slavery times (Lademann-Priemer 429).

In the following, I will return to a comparison between Kongolese and voodooist's community life. Historical research reveals that the king of Kongo (by members referred to as nkisi) was the head of the region, and responsible for benedictions (MacGaffey 195), the community's well-being, and weather conditions. He was also called "Nzambi a Mpungu" meaning "superior to all other nzambi" (197). Besides him was the Simbi priest called "kitomi", who held the role of a prophet (197) and took care of the community's well-being. He practiced his cult independently from the king, and every region had its priest whose dedicated wife assisted him in his functions (195). Subordinates to the king and priests lived close to them. Members of families who were related by their fathers were able to assign to each other's traditions and addressed as "children and grandchildren" (26).

In a similar vein, voodoo communities see themselves as spiritual families. Accordingly, each community has a leading priest called "oungan" or priestess called "mambo" (Reuter 33). Like in Kongo communities, the followers are seen as "children" to the priest and practitioners use the terms "mama" and "papa" to address them (33). A reasonable parallel between the addressing of "mama" and "papa" and "children and grandchildren" might be that Kongo and Louisiana had both previously been French territory, hence, spoke French. From a linguistical perspective, it might be the case that "mama" and "papa" derive from the French words "Mami" and "Papi", translated into the English terms "grandmother" and "grandfather" and, as a result, draws a connection between the Kongo cosmology and New Orleans Voodoo.

The Kongo cosmology further influenced symbolism in New Orleans voodoo, which can be demonstrated in certain symbols. Due to the lack of scholarly work, I will focus on the twin cult. One hallmark in Kongo cosmology was giving birth to unusual children, such as malformed, albinos, or twins. According to the BaKongo belief, these children were the reincarceration of local spirits (MacGaffey 85).

Especially twins were a two folded burden for their families. On one side, it was more difficult for mothers to feed to babies at the same time, and on the other side, the BaKongo believed that twins have supernatural powers, which they use to jinx one another or people they dislike (85). Furthermore, twins were said to be jealous of each other and therefore constantly in a fight ever since they shared their mother's womb, dizygotic twins even more than monozygotic twins because they came into existence from different waters (86).

Applying this perception, voodooists honor twins correspondingly in a few aspects. Like in the above portrayal, they also believe in the magical powers of twins and assume that they are jealous of each other and additionally very moody (Reuter 41). Although BaKongos observed twins as more like a burden, voodooist twin mothers have a special religious and family responsibility. Her two duties are first, to avoid jealousy and treat both twins permanently equally, and secondly, to honor the living and dead twins of her family regularly through ritual dinners (41).

Finally, I will outline parallels in the BaKongo concept of rituals and voodoo in New Orleans. The function of rituals in Kongo cosmology is to influence the world of the living and the dead (MacGaffey 6). By this, powers can be transferred from spirits to humans or members of the community can transcend into a different state (12). Priests were believed to have healing powers and therefore hold rites publicly (7), which were accompanied by singing and conjuration (12). Charms were primarily used to support individuals' fortune (137), however, there are also cursing charms that require a blood sacrifice to afflict witches (156). Besides, reptiles were associated with the transcendence of both worlds. Whereas crocodiles stood for death, snakes were honorable creatures and symbolized rebirth due to their ability to slip out of their skin (121).

New Orleans Voodoo rituals show similar elements of their practices. Like in Kongo, voodooists can change the conditions of state by the priest*ess, who prepares the voodooist for the ritual (Reuter 44). According to their belief, one loa descents to get control over the mind of the one in trance, while the actual mind wanders around outside of the body (44). As previously discussed, the BaKongo presume that souls can leave the body temporarily. The body of the obsessive voodooist stumbles and trembles while the community sings and dances (43), which resembles the singing and conjuring part of Kongo rituals. There are other voodoo ceremonies to adjure Li Grand Zombi by voodoo gris-gris, the pendant to Kongo charms, and the sacrifice of snakes (Britannica Marie Laveau). Even so, animal sacrifice is seldomly found in New Orleans Voodoo literature.

Unlike in Kongo cosmology, there is controversy about the reputation of snakes in New Orleans Voodoo. I observed a profound lack of reliable sources that deal with honoring or sacrificing snakes in New Orleans Voodoo, however, the great merit of the similar territorial conditions of Kongo and Louisiana, Kongolese slaves were able to practice rituals with familiar animals and adoption of reptiles and snake symbolism into the Voodoo culture.

I follow from what I said and conclude that Kongo religiosity and New Orleans Voodoo share meaningful elements, like the hierarchical system of gods and humans, community life, and death cult, as well as certain symbols and rituals. Significantly, I found additional parallels between both religiosities during my research, for example, specific dance rituals and a broad spectrum of Christian-Kongolese syncretism that originated in pre-transatlantic Kongo and might have influenced New Orleans Voodoo as well. However, due to the scope of this research paper and partly insufficient scholarly work considering New Orleans Voodoo as a particular subdivision of Haitian Vodou, I could not take them into account.

CONCLUSION

A central contention of this research paper was the existence of Kongolese religiosity in New Orleans Voodoo. Therefore, this paper aimed to discover characteristics that both religiosities have in common. I started with significant elements of New Orleans Voodoo and continued with the exhibition of religious movements of the Kongo kingdom to illustrate background information for the reader. Applying to this, I attempted to explain the reasons for the progress of Kongolese religiosity in New Orleans by connecting figures and circumstances of the transatlantic slave trade with slave conditions in Louisiana from a historical point of view. This proved that the transatlantic slave trade was mainly responsible for the demographic movement of Kongolese to Southern North America and the resulting religious influence on New Orleans Voodoo. Towards the end, my research demonstrated key components that appear in Kongo religiosity and New Orleans voodoo likewise. Further studies might help to shed light on rituals of New Orleans Voodoo explicitly distanced from Haitian Vodou, especially animal sacrifice, the portrayal of loas from a cosmological perspective, or the examination of similarities between trance- and ritual dances of New Orleans Voodoo in comparison to dance rituals from the Kongo kingdom.

Works Cited

Claudio, Mattes. "Voodoo." *Metzler-Lexikon Religion,* Metzler, Stuttgart, 2005, pp. 580–584.

Cooksey, Susan, et al. *Kongo across the Waters.* University Press of Florida, 2013.

Dewulf, Jeroen. "Sangamentos on Congo Square? Kongolese Warriors, Brotherhood Kings, and Mardi Gras Indians in New Orleans." *Afro-Catholic Festivals in the Americas: Performance, Representation, and the Making of Black Atlantic Tradition,* Pennsylvania State University Press, University Park, 2021, pp. 23–41.

Domingues da Silva, Daniel B. *The Atlantic Slave Trade from West Central Africa, 1780-1867.* Cambridge University Press, 2017.

Fandrich, Ina J. "Yorùbá Influences on Haitian Vodou and New Orleans Voodoo." *Journal of Black Studies,* vol. 37, no. 5, 2007, p. 775.

"Haitian Revolution" *Encyclopædia Britannica,* Encyclopædia Britannica, Inc., https://www.britannica.com/topic/Haitian-Revolution (Accessed August 17th, 2022)

Heusch, Luc De. "Kongo in Haiti: A New Approach to Religious Syncretism." *Man [new Series].,* vol. 24, no. 2, 1989.

Johnson, Jerah. "New Orlean's Congo Square: An Urban Setting for Early Afro-American Culture Formation." *Louisiana History: The Journal of the Louisiana Historical Association,* vol. 32, no. 2, 1991, pp. 117–157.

Lademann-Priemer, Gabriele. *Voodoo.* Originalausg. Herder, 2011.

Long, Carolyn Morrow. "Perceptions of New Orleans Voodoo: Sin, Fraud, Entertainment, and Religion." *Nova Religio: The Journal of Alternative and Emergent Religions,* vol. 6, no. 1, 2002, pp. 86-101.

MacGaffey, Wyatt. *Religion and Society in Central Africa.* Univ. of Chicago Press, 1986.

"Marie Laveau." *Encyclopædia Britannica*, Encyclopædia Britannica, Inc., https://www.britannica.com/biography/Marie-Laveau (accessed August 17th, 2022)

Reuter, Astrid. *Voodoo*. Orig.-Ausg. Beck, 2003.

Touchstone, Blake. "Voodoo in New Orleans." *Louisiana History: The Journal of the Louisiana Historical Association*, vol. 13, no. 4, 1972, p. 371.

Voss, Jelmer. "Kongo, North American, and the Slave Trade." *Kongo across the Waters*, University Press of Florida, Gainesville, 2013, pp. 40–49.

YOUR KNOWLEDGE HAS VALUE

- We will publish your bachelor's and
  master's thesis, essays and papers

- Your own eBook and book -
  sold worldwide in all relevant shops

- Earn money with each sale

Upload your text at www.GRIN.com
and publish for free